BE YOUR BEST

# GRIT

Shannon Welbourn

AV2

www.av2books.com

AV2

**Step 1**
Go to **www.av2books.com**

**Step 2**
Enter this unique code

**FAXTKJ1M5**

**Step 3**
Explore your interactive eBook!

AV2 is optimized for use on any device

# Your interactive eBook comes with...

**Contents**
Browse a live contents page to easily navigate through resources

**Audio**
Listen to sections of the book read aloud

**Videos**
Watch informative video clips

**Weblinks**
Gain additional information for research

**Try This!**
Complete activities and hands-on experiments

**Key Words**
Study vocabulary, and complete a matching word activity

**Quizzes**
Test your knowledge

**Slideshows**
View images and captions

## ... and much, much more!

BE YOUR BEST

# GRIT

## Contents

# What Is Grit?

**Can you think about a time in your life when you became discouraged, or felt like giving up? Did you find a way to finish what you started? Or were you stopped in your tracks?**

Grit is a **mindset** that includes the character qualities of **persistence** and **determination**. It is also being **resilient** and strong despite any **obstacles** that you encounter. People with grit finish what they start and resist giving up. Everyone has the ability to develop grit.

**The challenges we face can become opportunities to build grit.**

Each time things do not go exactly how we want, we have an opportunity. We can feel discouraged and sad, or we can show our strength and determination. How we learn and grow from these challenges helps us to develop grit. Each time we fail and try again, our grit becomes stronger.

## Learn to Make Decisions

What is something in your life that could **benefit** from a gritty **attitude**?

# Grit Grows Goals!

**Grit helps you to succeed in different parts of your life.**

When you set out to do something, you have a goal in mind. A goal is something you want to achieve. Sometimes you are successful on your first try. Other times, it takes many tries to reach your goal. Failing and having the determination to keep trying until you reach your goal is what makes you gritty. Grit can take time to develop. You will work on building grit throughout your life.

You grow and develop each time you do not reach your goal but decide to try again. This is called **perseverance**. When you try again, you get stronger and more resilient. Each time you try, you learn more about who you are. Learning to be gritty is important, so do not give up!

**We build grit each time we fall down and get back up.**

BIOGRAPHY

# Climax-Fisher Knights

**The girls' basketball team from Climax-Fisher High School is an amazing example of grit.**

The team had been on a losing streak from 2011 to 2014. Over the years, they had lost a total of 84 straight games! That did not stop the coach from inspiring the players, and it did not stop the girls from trying their hardest. The players showed their love for the game. They displayed grit by working together as a team and not giving up. Even in the 85th game, when five players **fouled out** and only three players were left on the court, they did not give up. The Knights stuck together and believed in each other. The game went into double overtime and the girls won, breaking the 84-game losing streak!

NAME: **Climax-Fisher Knights**
FROM: **Fisher, Minnesota**
ACCOMPLISHMENT:
**Did not give up and accomplished their goal... on the 85th try!**

Even after so many losses, the girls of the Climax-Fisher Knights persevered by working together and following their passion, or love, for the game.

Climax-Fisher Knights won their 85th game by a score of

**62-58**.

Climax-Fisher Knights once lost a game by a score of

**90-3**.

The **three** girls left on the court were the **least experienced** players on the team.

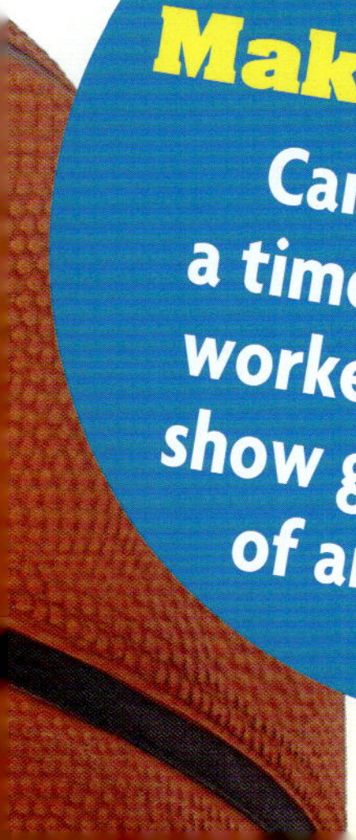

## Learn to Make Decisions

Can you think of a time that you have worked in a team to show grit in the face of an obstacle?

# Grit at Home

**Can you think of a time that you used grit at home? Family members can all work together to build grit.**

Families sometimes have to take on big tasks together. You and your family are spending a weekend cleaning out the garage. There are a lot of old toys and tools in there! You would rather be spending the weekend playing with friends, but you made a **commitment** to help clean the garage and your family is counting on you.

Following through to finish what you start helps build grit. It also shows others that they can depend on you.

Even though cleaning out the garage is a difficult job, you show grit when you stick with your commitment and help your family finish the task. When everyone works together to get things finished, you show grit as a family!

# Grit at School

**At school, we can build grit every day. By persevering and working hard even when things are difficult, we develop grit and succeed at school.**

We can be faced with many challenges throughout the day at school. Most kids find schoolwork difficult from time to time, especially when they are learning something new. Think about a time that you felt frustrated learning something new. You might have felt like giving up, but it is important to persevere and keep trying. Even though you might get the wrong answer sometimes, trying again builds grit at school.

Showing grit means trying different **strategies** until you get it right.

You are working on a project with a partner in science class. You need to build a model bridge that can hold up a 5-pound (2.3-kilogram) weight. Every time you test your bridge, the weight falls through! It could be easy to feel discouraged, but you and your partner decide to keep trying different designs for the bridge until one works. When you keep trying, you learn how to figure out problems and you develop grit.

# Grit in Your Community

**A community is a group of people who live, work, and play in a place. Your home, school, and neighborhood are part of your community.**

You can show and build grit in your community in many different ways. You could build grit by helping to clean up the local park every Saturday or growing flowers in a community garden, even if they wilt when it is too hot outside.

**You might decide to run in a race for charity. You can show your determination by spending the weeks before the race raising money for the charity. Then, you complete the race even when it gets hard and you feel tired. That is true grit!**

Maybe you are part of the baseball team in your community. You set a goal for yourself to make one run every game. Setting a goal for yourself can help you build grit because even when you face challenges, your goal can keep you focused. Grit helps you to keep going until you reach your goal.

**Keep trying. Keep practicing. Your results will show your hard work and grit.**

**"I can accept failure. Everyone fails at something. But I cannot accept not trying again."**

—Michael Jordan
Pro basketball player

BIOGRAPHY

# Abdul Muqeet

**At the age of 8, Abdul Muqeet learned that plastic bags cause serious pollution. Passionate about helping the environment, Abdul has used his unstoppable grit to help stop the use of plastic bags.**

When Abdul's teacher announced that his class would be having a "no plastic day" in October 2010, Abdul decided to learn why he should avoid using plastic. He discovered that plastic can be harmful to the environment and decided he would work to fix the problem. Abdul created bags out of paper instead of plastic to help people in his community stop using plastic bags when shopping. He worked very hard to make the bags himself out of recycled newspaper.

NAME: **Abdul Muqeet**
FROM: **Abu Dhabi, United Arab Emirates**
ACCOMPLISHMENT:
**Followed his passion for the environment to help get rid of plastic bags**

Although it took time, Abdul did not give up on his goal. Many years later, Abdul still follows his passion to save the environment and solve pollution problems in his country and around the world. He uses his grit to continue to make paper bags and encourage recycling. With a little creativity and a lot of grit, Abdul is inspiring people everywhere to live in a more environmentally friendly way.

It can take up to

**1,000**

years for a plastic bag to break down in a landfill.

Every year, about

**100 billion**

billion plastic bags are used in the United States alone.

**"A small step in our day-to-day life can make a big difference to the environment. It is our sole responsibility to care for Planet Earth and make it a better place to live."**

—Abdul Muqeet

Only

**1 percent**

of the plastic bags used in the United States each year are recycled.

# Overcoming Challenges

**Having grit comes down to a mindset. Your thoughts and actions are what build grit.**

Think of the well-known quote, "If at first you do not succeed, try, try again." When something does not go your way, do not give up. When you need a bit of grit to help you succeed, try these tips:

- Sometimes we can lose focus or get discouraged. Do not let this be an obstacle! Remember your goals and why they matter to you to help you keep trying.
- Look at what you are doing and review your plan of action. Should you try a different strategy?
- Learn each time and adjust your strategies as needed. Each attempt should get you closer to your goal.

Sometimes you have to fail in order to succeed. Think about a time you did not reach your goal. How did this make you feel? You are in control of how you let failure affect you. Should you get discouraged and give up, or use it as a way to learn, improve, and try again? You can learn to look at failures as challenges, and view challenges as opportunities. This will help you develop a gritty mindset.

**Learn to Make Decisions**

What advice would you give someone who has experienced failure?

# Encouraging Grit in Others

**Once you have figured out how to develop your gritty mindset, you can help others, too!**

Encourage others to build their mindset for grit as well. If you see someone showing grit, encourage them to keep going. When you see someone fail or get discouraged, you can encourage grit by cheering them on! Encourage them to not give up. Show others how to persevere by working hard to achieve your goals, no matter the challenges in your way. Encourage others to keep positive and to show determination. When you believe in something, it is easier to keep going. You have to believe you can do it, even when others may not. Help others to see that they have grit, too! Be gritty!

When you show others that you believe in them, you are helping them to believe in themselves. That builds grit!

# Grit in Action

**Grit can help you reach your goals now and in the future!**

To keep your grit on track, pay attention to your thoughts and actions and make sure they support a gritty mindset. Use the statements below to help you see the ways you show grit and areas where you can work to build more grit in your life. There are no right or wrong answers. Use this page again and again in the future to help make sure you keep stepping forward with grit!

**Read each statement. How well does it describe you? Think about your recent thoughts and actions to help you decide.**

I finish what I am working on before starting something new.

I can give a lot of effort and time to things that I think are interesting and important.

I use many different strategies to reach my goals.

When I make a mistake, I think about what I can learn from it.

I can deal with setbacks and obstacles. I do not get too discouraged or give up.

# Key Words

**attitude:** a feeling, mood, or way of thinking
**benefit:** an advantage or something that is good
**commitment:** a promise to do something
**determination:** the quality of being firm, or having strength of mind and character
**fouled out:** in basketball, to be removed from a game after committing too many fouls against other players
**mindset:** an intention, attitude, or mood
**obstacles:** things or events that get in the way
**perseverance:** persistence in a course of action despite difficulties
**persistence:** determined continuance of action
**resilient:** recovering or springing back after a challenge
**strategies:** plans for achieving a goal

# Index

Published by AV2
350 5th Avenue, 59th Floor
New York, NY 10118
Website: www.av2books.com



Library of Congress Control Number: 2020937050

ISBN 978-1-7911-2799-2 (Hardcover)
ISBN 978-1-7911-2800-5 (Softcover)
ISBN 978-1-7911-2801-2 (Multi-user eBook)
ISBN 978-1-7911-2802-9 (Single-user eBook)

Printed in Guangzhou, China
1 2 3 4 5 6 7 8 9 0 24 23 22 21 20

042020
101119

Project Coordinator: Sara Cucini Designer: Jean Faye Marie Rodriguez

Every reasonable effort has been made to trace ownership and to obtain permission to reprint copyright material. The publishers would be pleased to have any errors or omissions brought to their attention so that they may be corrected in subsequent printings.

The publisher acknowledges Getty Images, iStock, Dreamstime, and Shutterstock as its primary image suppliers for this title.

First published by Crabtree Publishing Company in 2017.